DOGON

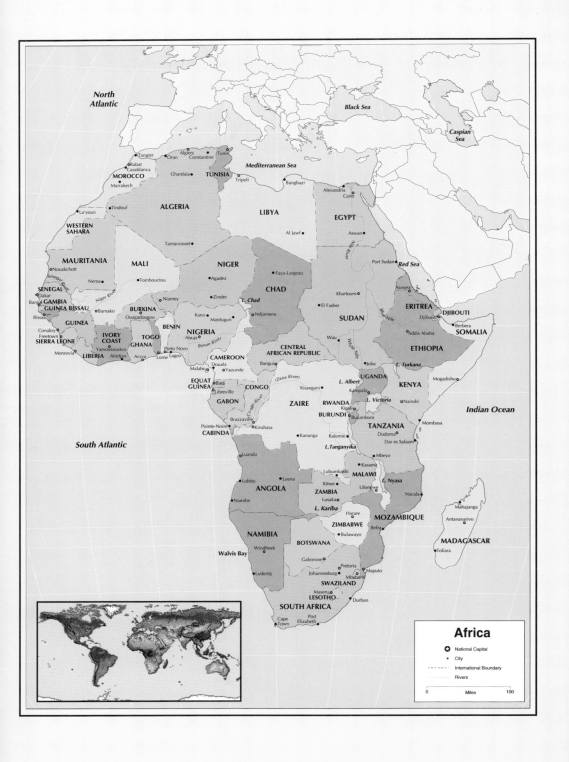

North
Atlantic

Black Sea

Caspian
Sea

Tangier
Rabat
Casablanca
MOROCCO
Marrakech
Oran
Algiers
Constantine
Tunis
TUNISIA
Ghardaia
Tripoli

Mediterranean Sea

Banghazi
Alexandria
Cairo

La'youn
Tindouf
ALGERIA
LIBYA
EGYPT

WESTERN
SAHARA

Al Jawf
Aswan

MAURITANIA
Nouakchott
MALI
NIGER
CHAD

Tamanrasset

Port Sudan
Red Sea
Nema
Tombouctou
Agadez
Faya-Largeau
Asmera

SENEGAL
Dakar
GAMBIA
GUINEA BISSAU
Bamako
Niamey
Zinder
L. Chad
Ndjamena
Khartoum
El Fasher
SUDAN
ERITREA
Djibouti
DJIBOUTI
Berbera

Bissau
Conakry
Freetown
GUINEA
BURKINA
Ouagadougou
Kano
Maiduguri
SOMALIA

SIERRA LEONE
IVORY
COAST
Yamoussoukro
TOGO
GHANA
BENIN
Abuja
NIGERIA
Benue River
Wau
White Nile
Blue Nile
Addis Abeba
ETHIOPIA

Monrovia
LIBERIA
Abidjan
Accra
Lome
Porto Novo
Lagos
CAMEROON
Douala
Yaounde
Bangui
CENTRAL
AFRICAN REPUBLIC
Juba
L. Turkana
Mogadishu

Malabo
EQUAT.
GUINEA
Bata
Libreville
CONGO
(Zaire River)
Kisangani
L. Albert
UGANDA
Kampala
KENYA
Nairobi

GABON
Congo River
ZAIRE
RWANDA
Kigali
L. Victoria
Indian Ocean

Brazzaville
Pointe-Noire
Kinshasa
BURUNDI
Bujumbura
TANZANIA
Dodoma
Mombasa

CABINDA
Kananga
Kalemie
Dar es Salaam

South Atlantic

Luanda
L.Tanganyika
Mbeya

Lobito
Luena
Kasama
MALAWI
L. Nyasa
Nacala

Namibe
ANGOLA
Lubumbashi
Kitwe
ZAMBIA
Lusaka
Lilongwe

NAMIBIA
Windhoek
BOTSWANA
L. Kariba
Harare
ZIMBABWE
Bulawayo
MOZAMBIQUE
Beira
Mahajanga

Antananarivo
MADAGASCAR
Toliara

Walvis Bay
Luderitz
Gaborone
Pretoria
Johannesburg
Maputo
Mbabane
SWAZILAND
Maseru
LESOTHO
Durban

SOUTH AFRICA
Cape
Town
Port
Elizabeth

Africa

National Capital
City
International Boundary
Rivers

0   Miles   100

The Heritage Library of African Peoples

DOGON

Chukwuma Azuonye, Ph.D.

THE ROSEN PUBLISHING GROUP, INC.
NEW YORK

Published in 1996 by The Rosen Publishing Group, Inc.
29 East 21st Street, New York, NY 10010

First Edition

Manufactured in the United States of America

Library of Congress Cataloging-in-Publication Data

Azuonye, Chukwuma, 1945–
    Dogon / Chukwuma Azuonye. — 1st ed.
        p.   cm. — (The heritage library of African peoples)
    Includes bibliographical references and index.
    ISBN 0-8239-1976-5
    1. Dogon (African people)—History—Juvenile literature.   2. Dogon
(African people)—Social life and customs—Juvenile literature.
[1. Dogon (African people)]   I. Title.   II. Series.
DT551.45.D64A98   1995
966.23′0049635—dc20   94-45814
                                                                CIP
                                                                AC

Contents

Introduction 6

1. The Dogon: Cliff Dwellers
   of Bandiagara 9

2. Dogon Traditions and History 17

3. The Dogon Creation Story 24

4. Philosophy, Religion, and
   Rituals 35

5. Dogon Order 45

6. Achievements of Dogon
   Civilization 50

7. The Dogon Today 55

Glossary 59

For Further Reading 61

Index 62

INTRODUCTION

THERE IS EVERY REASON FOR US TO KNOW something about Africa and to understand its past and the way of life of its peoples. Africa is a rich continent that has for centuries provided the world with art, culture, labor, wealth, and natural resources. It has vast mineral deposits, fossil fuels, and commercial crops.

But perhaps most important is the fact that fossil evidence indicates that human beings originated in Africa. The earliest traces of human beings and their tools are almost two million years old. Their descendants have migrated throughout the world. To be human is to be of African descent.

The experiences of the peoples who stayed in Africa are as rich and as diverse as of those who established themselves elsewhere. This series of books describes their environment, their modes of subsistence, their relationships, and their customs and beliefs. The books present the variety of languages, histories, cultures, and religions that are to be found on the African continent. They demonstrate the historical linkages between African peoples and the way contemporary Africa has been affected by European colonial rule.

Africa is large, complex, and diverse. It encompasses an area of more than 11,700,000 square miles. The United States, Europe, and India could fit easily into it. The sheer size is an indication of the continent's great variety in geography, terrain, climate, flora, fauna, peoples, languages, and cultures.

Much of contemporary Africa has been shaped by European colonial rule, industrialization, urbanization, and the demands of a world economic system. For more than seventy years, large regions of Africa were ruled by Great Britain, France, Belgium, Portugal, and Spain. African peoples from various ethnic, linguistic, and cultural backgrounds were brought together to form colonial states.

For decades Africans struggled to gain their independence. It was not until after World War II that the colonial territories became independent African states. Today, almost all of Africa is ruled by Africans. Large numbers of Africans live in modern cities. Rural Africa is also being transformed, and yet its people still engage in many of their customs and beliefs.

Contemporary circumstances and natural events have not always been kind to ordinary Africans. Today, however, new popular social movements and technological innovations pose great promise for future development.

George C. Bond, Ph.D., Director
Institute of African Studies
Columbia University, New York

Dogon art is found in art museums throughout the world. In museums, objects such as these wooden masks, representing animals, are usually stripped of their fibres. Museums cannot capture the dramatic effect of a mask, which greatly depends on the costume and the dancer's movements.

1

THE DOGON: CLIFF DWELLERS OF BANDIAGARA

THE DOGON PEOPLE OF MALI AND BURKINA
Faso in the bend of the Niger River, known as
the Niger Bend, are among the most remarkable
peoples in the world. A nation of fewer than
400,000 people, they are nevertheless better
known than other more populous peoples of
Africa. They are famous for their colorful masks
(*imina*), symbolic wooden statues (*dege*), and
other art that has influenced modern art in
Europe and elsewhere. They are equally re-
nowned for their complex philosophy and
worldview and advanced scientific knowledge.

The Dogon are primarily a nation of grain
farmers. Most of them live in more than 700
small villages scattered over 15,000 square miles
in the Bandiagara region of north central Mali,
an area of high and colorful cliffs with many
natural caves. Some live on a sandstone plateau

above the cliffs, and the rest live in the vast, sandy plains below, an area called Senó that stretches into the northern frontiers of the neighboring Republic of Burkina Faso.

Until recently, Dogon country was isolated from the rest of the world. The founding fathers of the civilization deliberately chose this isolation. For centuries it protected them from attacks by outsiders, enabling them to safeguard their culture and values. Dogon country is easier to reach today. Roads have been built, and tourists flock to the country to view the strange beauty of the cliffs and caves and to watch traditional dances and masked plays adapted for their entertainment.

▼ COMMUNITY LIFE ▼

The main center of Dogon community life is the village. The Dogon village is patrilineal, that is, a community whose members trace their ancestry along the male line, but strong bonds also exist with mother's relatives. Each village is an independent social and political entity, but shares many cultural features with other villages.

Situated on the cliffs, the village of Sanga is the cultural capital of Dogon country. Other important villages are Songo, Kamba, Banani, Tenyu Ireli, Tireli, Amani, Nini, and Bandiagara, after which the region is named. Like Sanga,

The Dogon are settled on the plains in villages that often have mosques rising above the houses (top) and also in villages built into cliffs (bottom left). At the center of villages is a *ginna* (big house) where the village patriarchs live (bottom right).

many of these larger villages are turning into urban areas.

In Dogon architecture, not only are houses built to resemble the shape of a human being, but the masses of conical and rounded forms that go into their design make them look collectively like anthills. The Dogon village community works with the proverbial unity of an anthill, and the anthill is a major symbol of communal order in the Dogon story of creation.

Stone houses and mud granaries, both rectangular and circular, dominate the scene in all Dogon settlements. In keeping with the principle of twinship, which, as we shall see, dominates Dogon thinking, each settlement has two sections—an upper and a lower section.

In the open space in the middle of each village is a big house (*ginna* or *ginu na*). Here dwells the patriarch (*ginna bana*) of each of the extended families (also called *ginna*) that make up the village.

In many of the villages, especially those like Songo in which Islam has become the main religion, mosques are built in the same style as the *ginna*. Each village also has a common meeting place, *togu na* (great shelter), with smaller ones (simply called *togu*) for each extended family. The *togu* are rectangular buildings, each with eight pillars grouped in four pairs.

Dogon villages have a meeting place for men called *togu na*. This example is unusual because the pillars are made of rock rather than of wood.

▼ THE DOGON ECONOMY ▼

The mainstay of the Dogon economy is the cultivation of grains, especially fonio, sorghum (male and female), millet, corn, rice, and beans. These are among the eight main grains that are the staple foods and cash crops of the people, but are also spiritually important. They form a divine group that represents the original four pairs of human ancestors. Dogon myth says that these eight seeds are equally distributed at birth in the shoulder bones or clavicles of every person, and stresses that the production of these grains rests squarely on the shoulders of every Dogon.

Grains such as sorghum, millet, and rice are staple foods of the Dogon and regarded as spiritually significant.

In the same way, grains are frequently mentioned in the Dogon creation story as symbols of the origins and continuity of life. For instance, the germ of all life—the tiny cell out of which the entire universe is believed to have come into being—is compared to the smallest cultivated seed, fonio.

Annual festivals of grain harvesting are among the important Dogon rites of renewal. During the festival the earth is cleansed by the Hogon, the spiritual head of each Dogon district. The Hogon is believed to be a successor of one of the four Dogon ancestors through whom the original impure earth was cleansed by the cultivation of the female sorghum, *emme ya.*

Grains are cultivated mainly in the cliff area around Sanga. Thanks to higher rainfall and less rapid evaporation, this area has more fertile soil than the plateau and the surrounding plains. Granaries are everywhere. A special granary architecture has developed, featuring doors and locks decorated with images related to Dogon belief.

The Dogon raise cattle, sheep, and goats, and are regarded as excellent hunters.

The importance of animals is seen in the many Dogon masks that represent antelopes, bulls, buffaloes, monkeys, and crocodiles.

Not being situated near a river, the Dogon depend to a large extent on the closely related Bozo or Sorogo people for fish. Bozo myths say that eight *miri*—the smallest of all fishes—rest in the shoulders of every Bozo. The Bozo in turn depend on the Dogon for grains. This interdependence has given rise to a special type of alliance called *mangu.*

The Dogon developed unique styles and skills in weaving, leatherworking, smithing, metal casting, and wood carving that have become important economic resources. Like all Dogon products, these bear the imprint of the Dogon system of beliefs. Weaving and blacksmithing are

Blacksmiths are held in high regard, both respected and feared for their great knowledge.

of particular significance because of their special connections with the twin pair of heavenly agents of creation, called Nommo, from which the people believe they sprang. Dogon blacksmiths carve the powerful and famous Dogon masks.▲

chapter

2
DOGON TRADITIONS AND HISTORY

THE ORIGINS OF THE DOGON ARE UNCERTAIN.
In oral traditions differing legends claim that the
people's ancestors came from each of the four
cardinal points. The most popular of these
legends, however, holds that their ancestors were
Mande people who migrated to the present
homeland from the northwest.

The Mande are a very large grouping of
nations. About forty-four peoples in West Africa
claim Mande origins: peoples in countries
stretching from Mali to Senegal on the Atlantic
coast. The most prominent of these are the
Mandinka of Gambia, the Bamana of Mali, the
Nono and Soninke of Ghana, and the Mossi
and Malinke of Burkina Faso. Many of these
peoples are related to the Dogon in language,
customs, and ways of life. Some historians
regard the term Mande as referring to the idea

The Distribution of the Dogon people in the countries of
Mali and Burkino Faso. Lake Debo is not a solid permanent body
of water, but fluctuates greatly depending on rainfall in the region.

of common origins that the people feel bind
them together. But the word Mande means
"king's place" or "the residence of the king,"
suggesting that it may in fact have something to
do with the capital of a kingdom or an empire.
Many historians think that it may refer to the
capital of one of the great empires of medieval
West Africa, possibly the Ghana Empire of the
Soninke people.

▼ MYTH OF ORIGIN ▼

Taking the oral traditions and archaeological
facts together, historians have reconstructed the
history of the Bandiagara region and of the

Dogon as follows. The region was first inhabited by hunter-gatherers who lived in caves. Later, the area became a refuge for people fleeing from war, famine, and the violence that accompanied the spread of Islam. Thereafter, various groups from the north and northwest settled in the area, mainly for the security it offered.

The Dogon believe that their ancestors were among the many groups of Mande people who were forced to migrate after the breakup of the Ghana empire in the 1300s. According to Dogon myth, a crane guided them to the region. In antiquity, the Dogon believe, four semidivine ancestors descended from the sky in an ark or a boat sent by the creator, Amma. The ark landed not far from the village of Mopti, at Mount Gourao, near Lake Debo. These four ancestors were given female twins to enable them to increase and multiply. Their descendants later migrated to Mande. The return from Mande to the Bandiagara cliffs, guided by the crane, was therefore a homecoming.

The early Dogon migrants did not move into uninhabited territory. They displaced earlier settlers called the Tellem, whose civilization is believed to have influenced them in many ways. The Tellem were also influenced by inhabitants they had displaced, known as the Toloy, named for the area where pottery, wooden sculpture, textiles, and other relics of their civilization have

Found in some of the caves in the spectacular cliffs of Dogon country are sculptures and other remains of the Tellem people who lived in this area before the Dogon.

recently been found by archaeologists. Thus, Dogon civilization combines the Mande heritage with traditions of the earlier Bandiagara inhabitants. Writers on Dogon art often distinguish between Dogon style and styles developed by the earlier inhabitants.

▼ DOGON CIVILIZATION ▼
The ancestors of the Dogon appear to have brought the Mande worldview, philosophy, and religion with them. Other aspects of Dogon culture seem to have been taken from the Tellem, and through them from the Toloy.

Between the 1500s and the 1800s, when the

French began to penetrate the Bandiagara area, the Dogon remained isolated. They developed a strong warrior tradition as a means of ensuring their independence. Over the centuries, they successfully beat off invasions and slave raids from Arabs and groups acting for European slave dealers on the coast.

After the African continent was divided up in Berlin among the rival European powers in 1885, the French made several forays into Dogon country. Their aim was to establish their authority in the territories that were awarded to them—the French Sudan (present-day Mali) and Upper Volta (present-day Burkina Faso). By the late 1800s, the French were firmly in control of Dogon country, and thereafter things began to fall apart for the Dogon and their highly advanced civilization.

▼ FRENCH RULE ▼

Under French rule, the Dogon continued to oppose foreign influences on their culture and society. They fought all missionary activity, considering their belief system to be superior to and more humane than Christianity. Revolting at every opportunity against the French and their agents, the Dogon have been described by historians as "one of the last peoples to lose their independence and come under French rule." The French were surprised by the stiff resistance

Elders, such as these two men, are highly respected in Dogon society.

of the Dogon. Constantly fearing revolts, the French kept a strict eye on the Dogon and often led punitive expeditions against them. Often they punished whole villages, and in some cases engaged in massacres.

French scholars developed a strong interest in the Dogon. This intensified when the first French visitors saw the unique beauty of the cliffs and the numbers of extraordinary sculptures and masks in the area. In the 1930s the Dakar-Djibouti research trip led by Marcel Griaule resulted in a better understanding of the Dogon culture. The opening up of the country to tourists began a process of change that has greatly affected the continuity and growth of Dogon traditions. Continued resistance to the French appears to have led those Dogon who abandoned their traditional religion to adopt Islam rather than Christianity.▲

chapter

3

THE DOGON CREATION STORY

DOGON ORAL TRADITION IS FULL OF STORIES of the origins of things. Although told separately, together they can be regarded as composing the Dogon creation story.

▼ THE SEED OF THE WORLD ▼

In the beginning, there was a very tiny seed, the seed of the world, so small that it can be compared only to "the smallest of things." It may be likened to an atom or a cell in the body of a living thing. The Dogon compare it to the fonio seed—very much like the mustard seed mentioned in the New Testament: the smallest of all seeds which, when it grows, becomes greater than all herbs. Before life appeared in the universe, this tiny seed floated about in the empty darkness of space. Despite its size, it contained everything we now know to exist in the world, including the sun and other stars, the earth and other planets, our moon and other moons, God and the gods, people, animals, plants, minerals, and everything else, living and nonliving. It was the germ or cell of all creation. Then came the big bang.

▼ THE DOGON BIG BANG ▼

When the seed of the world had drifted to the place in the heavens where the brightest star, the Dog Star, Sirius A, and its dwarf companion, Sirius B, are located, the seed of the world was suddenly forced to explode by powerful vibrations inside it. The explosion was like the splitting of the nucleus of an atom. The contents of the seed expanded and expanded until they filled all space, reaching the utmost confines of the universe.

Then the contents formed a large oval mass, the egg of the world (*aduno tal*). This was the egg out of which all created life was to emerge, when the embryo of the world was ready to be born.

▼ THE EGG OF THE WORLD ▼

The Dogon say that the movement of the expanding contents of the seed of the world occurred along a spiral path that is represented in Dogon drawings by a zigzag line (*ozu tonolu*). We know today that chromosomes, which carry

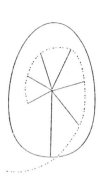

The first seven vibrations in the egg of the world (after Griaule and Dieterlen, 1965).

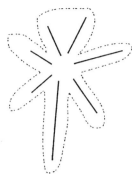

The refiguration of the human shape in the egg of the world (Griaule and Dieterlen, 1965).

the genes containing instructions for the making of each new life, have this spiral or helix shape.

This unwinding spiral movement is said to have taken place in seven vibrations, each longer than the one before it. At the seventh vibration the envelope broke, releasing all creation into outer space just as life hatches from an egg.

▼ THE HUMAN SHAPE ▼

The Dogon believe that the world was created in the interests of human beings. Second, they see human beings as the center of the wonders of creation. Third, all creation began in the egg-womb of the world just as a human baby is formed in its mother's womb. It is not surprising, therefore, that the creation story says that after the egg of the world broke open the contents took on the human shape.

In line with the idea that the human shape was contained within the egg of the world, the

The "egg of the world" is recalled in many aspects of Dogon culture,
such as the shape of this earth altar.

Dogon design their homes and the layout of
farmlands so that they echo the human shape.
The idea that human beings are the center of
the universe encourages the belief that whatever
happens to any person in this world affects the
larger society and the earth and universe as a
whole. This philosophy encourages respect for
the life of every human being, no matter how
small, as part of the life of the universe.

▼ SYMBOLS OF LIFE? ▼

Returning to happenings in the egg or womb
of the world, it may be that the Dogon saw a

code for all life in what they call *yala*. The *yala* are images or "written signs" or codes that stand for 22 different kinds of life into which the Dogon group everything that exists.

Within the egg of the world, the 22 *yala* were written on a plate that was divided into four sections, each ruled by one of the four elements—air, water, earth, and fire. As the first vibrations of the egg occurred, the *yala* were flung into space as the plate turned on itself. Each fell on the category of life to which it corresponded and brought that category to life.

▼ THE TWENTY-TWO BASIC CATEGORIES ▼

The two best-known writers on Dogon life and culture, Marcel Griaule and his pupil, Germaine Dieterlen, write as follows about the *yala* and the 22 basic categories: "All these images seem to relate to an effort of discovery, an attempt to apprehend the infinitely small at its point of departure towards the immeasurably vast. In fact, the order of the heavens, as it is observed by the Dogon, is no more than a projection, infinitely expanded, of events and phenomena that occur in the infinitely small" (1965, p. 85).

This is a very important observation. The Dogon creation story explains the creation of the universe in the light of their knowledge of how

The dance of *kanaga* masks, shown here, includes spiral movements of the masks that imitate the creation of the universe. "*Kanaga*" means "the hand of God in creating the world."

human life is created in the womb. If this is so, then the 22 basic categories must be understood in terms of the biology of human reproduction. The *yala*, which gave life, are strikingly similar to what scientists today call the genetic code. The 22 *yala* may be compared to 22 of the 23 pairs of human chromosomes that carry the genes that are the codes of life; the 23rd pair of human chromosomes determines a person's gender. Interestingly, while the 22 *yala* are grouped into four sections, DNA is controlled by four bases: adenine, thymine, guanine, and cytosine. The Dogon creation story contains knowledge that is thus similar to modern scientific knowledge.

▼ AMMA AND THE NOMMO ▼

The first of the 22 basic categories to emerge as conscious beings were the deities. The chief deity, Amma, became the god of creation. He undertook to complete or continue the work of creation as a great father-figure, procreating and putting things in order.

At first, Amma attempted to create things directly. But after meeting with some serious failures, he proceeded more cautiously. He created a pair of twins, called Nommo, the godly ancestors of human beings. They were half-human, half-snake, with red eyes and green bodies. Nommo are often described by the Dogon people as "the offspring of God," "water god," "master of water," "God's agent," "God's emanation," and "prefiguration of human." One male, one female, the Nommo are represented in Dogon statues of standing couples, each with male and female attributes.

The Nommo were sent down to create the world anew, to remove all impurities. Through these perfect twins, Amma had already created the sky and the stars to perfection. They would now create a new earth, one that would be perfect. They came down from the sky in a gigantic ark that the Dogon describe as "the Ark of the World." It is also called "the Granary of the Master of Pure Earth." Contained in it was everything needed to create a *gana duge* (a world in harmony). Piloted by the two heavenly Nommos, who now took the guise of two blacksmiths, the Ark of the World finally came to rest in the present location of the earth, where it instantly became a complete new earth. Until then the universe had been in total darkness. Now light appeared and rain that cleansed and purified the earth, making it ready for the first ancestors of human beings.

With the descent of Nommo came not only the separation of earth from other planets, but also the separation of night from day and the appearance of the cycle of the moon (months) and of seasons, years, and generations. Social

The Nommo descended to earth in an ark that the Dogon call the Granary of the Master of Pure Earth. They purified the earth and made it ready for agriculture. Dogon granaries, such as this one, thus have religious associations. A carved wooden ladder with upturned arms is placed below the window.

life was organized, and the artistic and technological foundations of civilization were laid by
the Nommo–turned–blacksmiths.

▼ THE MASTER BLACKSMITH ▼

Though an evil being, Yurugu the Master
Blacksmith is still remembered in Dogon
rituals today for the theft of a piece of the sun.
Through his act, he brought fire to the world.
Fire made art and technology possible. He
taught humans to weave, make music and musi-
cal instruments, and to make agricultural and
household implements.

▼ THE FIRST HUMAN ANCESTORS ▼

The first ancestors of human beings appeared
soon after the descent of the Ark of the World or
the Granary of the Master of Pure Earth.
According to the Dogon creation story, four
Nommo soon arrived from the East, West,
North, and South. They gave birth to eight
ancestors: four males, Amma Seru, Lébé Seru,
Binu Seru, and Dyongu Seru, each with a female companion, his sister and wife. These eight
ancestors brought with them eight seeds that
they planted in the pure and fertilized earth.
Out of each seed, a new seed grew.

On the new earth a civilization blossomed in
which the value of human life was governed by
ideas of the completeness and meaningfulness of

human life. These ideas are the basis of the challenging philosophy, religion, and rituals of continuity and renewal for which the Dogon have become widely known.▲

The Dogon have a rich heritage and have experienced many changes. While there may be a large gap in the experiences of this grandfather and child, many Dogon elders hope that core traditions will be preserved.

chapter

4

PHILOSOPHY, RELIGION, AND RITUALS

THE DOGON CREATION STORY CONTAINS, IN poetic language, a highly complex system of thought. The influence of this philosophy is found not only in the people's religion but in every aspect of their daily life. It is seen in their customs, names, daily greetings, architecture, weaving, carving and other arts, and in their systems of law and government. It is difficult for an outsider to make sense of anything in the Dogon way of life without understanding the main aspects of their philosophy.

In general, the Dogon make a distinction between two broad categories of knowledge, namely *giri so* ("front speech" or elementary knowledge of the world), and *so dayi* ("clear speech" or advanced knowledge arrived at through revelation and progressive initiation).

In many ways, being initiated into *so dayi* is

like formal schooling, from elementary school through middle and high schools to university. The process can consume a lifetime and takes place in four stages. It begins with *giri so* (front speech) and proceeds through the stages of *benne so* (side speech) and *bolo so* (back speech) to the final stage of perfect understanding of the world that the people call *so dayi*. As the name implies, everything becomes clear. But *so dayi*, according to the Dogon, includes so much that affects the universe as a whole that it should not be revealed to all and sundry.

For several centuries, the Dogon succeeded in guarding *so dayi* from all outsiders. It was not until the 1930s that some aspects of their knowledge were revealed. This occured through the blind hunter and sage Ogotemmeli, who held a series of conversations with the French ethnographer Marcel Griaule. According to Griaule, Ogotemmeli "laid bare the framework of a world system," the knowledge of which Griaule thought would revolutionize Western understanding of Africa.

Griaule remarked that although the full range of Ogotemmeli's teaching is known only to the Dogon elders and to certain initiates, it is not secret, since anyone who reaches old age can acquire *so dayi*. Since Ogotemmeli, many other aspects of *so dayi* have been discussed with Western researchers. We now know that the advanced knowledge of Dogon *so dayi* is founded on four major pillars that explain the science of the universe.

▼ FOUR PILLARS OF DOGON PHILOSOPHY ▼

Stated briefly, the four pillars of Dogon philosophy are: first, that the universe is a system of forces (*dynamism*); second, that human beings are the centerpiece of all creation and hence that everything in the universe is viewed from a human perspective (*anthropocentricism*); third, that everything in existence comes in balanced pairs or twins (*dualism*); and fourth, that everything in the universe represents a miniature of the whole (*microcosmicism*).

Dynamism (the idea that the universe is a system of forces) is a fairly universal philosophy. It is widespread among African peoples. Force implies motion; it is power that breaks inertia and keeps things moving. It is also power that can bring moving objects back to rest. The Dogon see this force in its most positive form as *nyama*, the vital force that set the seed of the world in motion. It became personified in Amma, the creator, and from Amma was transmitted to all beings.

At death, *nyama* is released and must be contained or it may cause harm. The Dogon do this by making images (*dege*) into which the *nyama* of the dead must be channeled. The main cer-

Dogon men fire blank charges to scare off spirits the day after a person's death.

Dogon women perform a dance on a rooftop the day following a person's death. The Dogon believe that *nyama*, the vital force of the universe, is released at death and must be carefully channeled to maintain harmony. Funeral activities such as these help clear *nyama*; while sculptures are used to contain it.

emonies of the Dogon are concerned with maintaining *nyama* in its positive forms and controlling all its negative forms.

The second pillar of Dogon philosophy, *anthropocentrism*, is the idea that human beings are the most perfect of all creations; therefore human beings present the image of the universe in its ideal form. It is also this form that one expects to see at all other levels of existence. Thus, ideally, the village, the larger human community, and the world are expected to imitate the human shape.

Dualism, the third pillar of Dogon philosophy, holds that all things must come in pairs. It derives from the idea that the original vibrations that led to creation took the form of a spiral or helical movement. This helical movement, represented by the zigzag line (*ozu tonnolo*), refers to the perpetual alternation of all opposite forces in the universe: male and female, south and north, hot and cold, etc. This alternation of opposite forces is seen as the basis of the self-perpetuation of the world through procreation.

Related to this dualism is the idea of perfect balance. One line of force (positive or negative) is balanced by the other. Thus, anything that does not contain an element of its opposite is incomplete. A man is incomplete without a female *nyama*, and a woman is incomplete without a male *nyama*.

The fourth major pillar, *microcosmicism*, is the idea that everything in the universe is a microcosm or miniature of the whole. As one moves down from the universe to the worlds in it, and from there to human societies at various levels, then to human beings, and finally to other creations, one is bound to see the same basic form. This is believed to go beyond form; it also applies to how things work. For the Dogon, human life and social life reflect the working of the universe, and in the same way the world order depends on society and on individual human beings for its proper operation.

▼ ASPECTS OF DOGON RELIGION ▼

Dogon religion, based on the four pillars of the philosophy discussed above, seeks to control the flow of the life force, *nyama*, in the interest of humankind as the center of all creation. In Dogon ceremonies, altars, and images (*dege*) of gods and other powers, care is taken to represent the principle of twinship associated with cosmic harmony. One is reminded at every stage that in the smallest of things will be found the image of the universe, which in turn reflects the form and functioning of the human body.

Two main aspects of this religion stand out clearly. One is the directness of the relationship between every Dogon person and the creator, Amma. The second is the existence of similar direct relationships with other major bearers of *nyama* through four fundamental cults or religious institutions: the totemic cult (*Binu*), the cult of the earth deity (*Lébé*), the cult of ancestors, and the cult of masks (*imina*).

Rites associated with all these aspects of religion involve first, the use of sculptures (*dege*) representing the object of worship; second, the chanting of invocations or hymns (*toro*) of praise and petition; and third, the sacrifice of an animal or the making of an offering, usually on an altar called *ama* or *omono*. The altar usually features a statue showing the worshiper in a pose that indicates the reason the sacrifice or offering is being made. The use of altars of this kind in Dogon religion differentiates the Dogon and other Mande religious practices from others in Africa.

▼ CEREMONIES OF CONTINUITY ▼

Daily life in Dogon society is made up of a series of colorful ceremonies concerned with maintaining the order and balance of the world. The Dogon also practice rites of renewal, whose purpose is to renew the life force (*nyama*) that controls the universe at all levels.

The Dogon rites of continuity are of two types. The first are rites of passage that mark key moments in the life cycle from birth to death. The most important of these rites are funeral

DOGON MASKS

Masks (*imina*) are extremely important in Dogon culture because they are believed to be the most powerful means of containing the excess *nyama* (life force) with which the universe is filled. The types of mask are put at between 65 and 78. All are performed by members of the Society of Masks, Awa. Each Dogon village has its own *Awa*. Members mainly perform rites of continuity or renewal, like the *Sigui* ceremony, held every 60 years.

Like folktales, Dogon masks reflect the human world, the animal world, the spirit world, and the wider universe or cosmos beyond the earth. Indeed, the name *Awa* means "cosmos."

Masks representing peoples include Satimbe (the beautiful woman) and Fulani (the West African people of that name, whom the Dogon regard as imbued with power). The animal world is represented by a variety of masks in the shape of mammals, reptiles, and birds.

The motions of the universe are evoked by the stateliness of Kanaga masks (whose name literally means "the hand of God in creating the world"). Even more magnificent is the Sirige mask, a mask representing the stars or a series of galaxies.

One of the most important masks is the great mask, *agamaga*, which represents the spirits of the first generation of ancestors who are believed to have been turned into snakes at the end of their lives on earth. This long mask is never worn. Rather it is carried from the caves in which it is guarded by the elders to and from the ceremonies at which it is required.

Some Dogon masks appear on stilts. These masks represent the Dogon's neighbors, the Fulani, recognized by their distinctive coiffure and their command of Islamic writing, indicated by the writing materials held by the masquerader on the left.

ceremonies, which promote the continuity of the life force beyond death. The second type consists of ceremonies that form part of the cults of Binu, Lébé, Amma, and Dyongu. The most representative of these are the rites connected with the Cult of Binu, which exists to promote growth in all things.

▼ RITES OF RENEWAL ▼

The most important rite of renewal is the Sigui ceremony, held every sixty years. This period is based on Dogon observation of the stars Sirius A and B. Long before these stars were known to the West, the Dogon noted that it

The Dogon practice many rituals closely connected to their belief system. These men are beating iron gongs during a ceremony.

takes sixty years for the small, heavy star of Sirius B to orbit its companion Sirius A, the Dog Star. The Dogon believe the location of the Sirius stars to be the source of the creation of the universe, and that the sixty-year orbit is significant because it is the approximate gap in time between human generations—between the young and the old. The Sigui ceremony thus times the celebration of the renewal of human generations upon the rhythm of the Sirius stars. ▲

5

DOGON ORDER

THE DOGON IDEA OF THE ORGANIZATION OF the world is represented by a diagram that they call "the life of the world." The drawing contains two egg-shaped forms, the top one complete, the lower one open at the bottom. The two shapes are joined by a vertical line that reaches down almost to the open end of the lower egg. While the two eggs are joined by the vertical line, they are separated by a horizontal line. On the face of it, the drawing looks like a sketch of a human being.

"The Life of the World".

The figure is indeed intended to be a sketch of a human shape, but it is the figure of a human being as a microcosm or small mirror image of the world as a whole. It is the Dogon idea that the human form mirrors the entire universe, the earth, the society in which we live, and the family to which we belong. In turn, the family, the society, the earth, and the universe mirror the human form.

▼ ORGANIZATION OF THE UNIVERSE ▼

The Dogon creation story says that the original four pairs of twins gave birth to four male ancesors (Amma Seru, Dyongu Seru, Binu Seru, Lébé Seru). In their turn, these four ancestors became the fathers of the four major ethnic divisions of Dogon society (Arou, Dyon, Ono, Dommo) that flourished before French rule was imposed. Each of the four ethnic groups came from one of the four directional points (East, South, West, North) and was linked with one of the four elements (air, fire, water, earth). In their original environment of isolation, the Dogon saw themselves as the sole occupants of all space on earth and among the stars. Thus, they believed that the earth and the heavenly bodies and the three main worldy functions—power, agriculture, and trade—were shared among them.

Note that there are four ethnic groups and

The Dogon place great emphasis on marriage, and the unity of male and female is emphasized in Dogon philosophy. This Dogon marriage was recorded in Mali.

three functions. The number four represents the female; the number three represents the male. The sum of three and four (seven) stands for the human personality. Thus, the four groups representing femininity and the three functions representing masculinity are combined to reveal the balance needed for the effective functioning of human society.

The Dogon believe that this harmonious organization of the universe is repeated at every level, from the organization of land and space, to the village community, to the family, and to the individual.

▼ ORGANIZATION OF LAND AND SPACE ▼

Following the principle of the twin-ness of all things, villages within a district are grouped in pairs, the Upper village and the Lower village. The Upper village is regarded as heaven (Nommo); the Lower one, earth (Yurugu).

Within each of these two villages is a big house (*ginu na*), which serves as the village meeting place. This house too reflects the human shape of the village and the district. So too does each individual homestead; each house is designed to resemble a man lying on his right side beside a woman.

▼ THE DOGON SPIRITUAL HEAD ▼

Groups of related Dogon villages in the three larger of the four major divisions of Dogon country are headed by a spiritual leader called the Hogon. The fourth and smallest group, Arou, constitutes one district, also headed by a Hogon.

Before French colonization, the Hogon was a powerful force in the Dogon world. He was the representative of his people. He was also an agricultural chief, responsible for the periodic cleansing of the soil and its preparation for cultivation.

The Hogon was also believed to be an avatar of Nommo on earth, a personification of the universe, with power to control the seasons and

Dogon philosophy and religion are complex and affect everyday life, but there is always room for humor. This man is clowning with mudfish attached to his fingers.

the movement of the stars. These functions were represented in every detail of his daily life: in his clothing, homestead, and his ceremonial and economic functions.▲

chapter

6

ACHIEVEMENTS OF DOGON CIVILIZATION

THE DOGON THEORY OF THE ORIGIN OF THE universe is similar to the "Big Bang" theory that is widely believed by scientists today. According to this theory, the universe originated as a result of a violent explosion from a point source. For Dogon, this point source is the seed of the universe. If the Big Bang theory is correct, then Dogon beliefs about the universe were closer to the truth very much earlier than Western science.

The Dogon were also advanced in their knowledge of astronomy. Until the Renaissance in Europe, most societies believed that the earth was the center of the universe. It was even an article of faith in the Catholic Church. The Italian scientist Galileo (1564–1642) made scientific observations supporting the idea that the earth and other planets moved around the sun, a belief promoted by the Polish astronomer Nicolaus Copernicus (1473–1543). Galileo was forced by the Church to retract his conclusions, and the Church did not admit he was correct until quite recently.

But before Copernicus and Galileo, the Dogon people appear to have known that the earth traveled in orbit around the sun. It is clear that they also knew about other planets and even worlds outside our solar system. They knew of the Dog Star, Sirius A, and that its companion, Sirius B, was smaller but heavier and took sixty years to orbit Sirius A. The Sigui ceremony of renewal refers to various aspects of what the Dogon knew about these twin stars and worlds beyond our solar system.

▼ SOCIAL ORGANIZATION AND THE ▼ SOCIAL SCIENCES

The system of correspondences in Dogon thought between the universe and the human body also extends to the organization of people in society. Like individual human beings, the village, the larger society, and the Dogon world as a whole share in the life of the world and partake in its basic structure. Thus, the layouts of homes and villages and of cultivated land are made to look like human beings. The working of each structure is also like that of the human body. This view is founded on principles of harmony and environmental protection, the sanctity of life, and the promotion of peaceful coexistence between people, families, and other social groups as parts of the same living body. Today these are the principles that most people in the world believe everyone should follow.

▼ DOGON TECHNOLOGY ▼

Dogon technology covers many fields including the mining and processing of metals, cotton planting and processing into textiles, food storage, architecture, erosion control, and irrigation. It is essentially practical, related to the problems of the difficult environment of isolation.

The importance of metal technology to the Dogon is seen in the prominence of the blacksmith in their story of creation and the use of metal in their everyday life. Besides iron, Dogon smiths worked on copper alloys of bronze and brass as well as on gold, silver, zinc, and tin. Today, Dogon smiths work on aluminum as well.

Dogon excellence in textile technology is related to their environment. Long before the industrial revolution in Europe, the growing of cotton featured so strongly in Dogon industry that the image of the weaver and his shuttle became one of the most powerful themes in Dogon arts. African textile technology and industry may have contributed to the development of the cotton and textile industry in the West in the era of slavery.

▼ DOGON ICONOGRAPHY ▼

It is often assumed that the peoples of Africa south of the Sahara became literate only after their contact with Arabs or Europeans. This is not true. The Dogon civilization, in addition to its meaningful ceremonies, had its own system of writing. This system is closely related to but different from the people's system of drawings and marking during religious ceremonies. In this sense, one can speak of indigenous literacy among the Dogon. Its extent is difficult to judge because it was never a popular form of expression. As a written form of clear speech (*so dayi*), it circulated mainly among initiates.

Dogon iconography—the drawing of signs—comprises the meaningful images or symbolic icons (*yala*) in a wide variety of media that express the main tenets of Dogon beliefs. Marks made on sculpture in wood, metal, or terra cotta and the shapes, numbers, and other features of these signs all convey ideas and often tell a story. In this way, iconography, though not exactly writing as such, can serve as a means of telling a story or communicating ideas as writing does.

▼ **THE ARTS OF THE DOGON** ▼

The most famous art form of the Dogon is their sculpture in wood, copper alloys, and iron, which generally represent the main themes of their creation story. Most powerful and expressive are their masks and images of the twin Nommo who are the perfect model of all creation.

Dogon aesthetics makes an interesting connection between the arts of weaving, music, and speech and the vital force *nyama*, which sustains the universe. The art of weaving is said to have been brought to humankind by the seventh Nommo, the Master Blacksmith. He also instructed them in music and speech, which are seen as the same substance. The root *mi* (harmony) occurs in the Dogon words for each of them. Like weaving, the movement of the sounds of both music and speech are said to follow the same spiral or zigzag movement that produced the egg of the world.▲

chapter

7

THE DOGON TODAY

MANY CHANGES ARE GOING ON IN DOGON culture and society today. Since the country has been opened to foreign influences, many Dogon have increasingly turned away from their traditional system of thought and their colorful ceremonies, arts, and way of life. The major factors in these changes include Islam and Christianity, Western values and technology, and, above all, tourism.

Because of the dominant place of Islam in the modern republics of Mali and Burkina Faso, the Dogon have increasingly converted to Islam. Many Dogon religious practices have been abandoned as "pagan." For instance, in the village of Songo, which is now Muslim, masked dances have not been performed for nearly three decades, and many young people know nothing about them. The blacksmiths who once carved

55

Today many Dogon are involved in the development and government of the modern countries in which they live.

masks no longer do so. They rather produce granary doors decorated with traditional motifs to sell to tourists. Many believe that the rapid growth of tourism has adversely affected traditional art forms. In the area of Sanga on the Bandiagara cliffs, masked dances and ceremonies have been adapted to suit the tastes of foreign consumers. Some say the masks have the color and shape of the originals but lack their meaning and significance.

Such critics believe that Dogon civilization has been damaged by the imposition of Islam and European colonial rule on Africa.

In remote villages many Dogon traditions continue to be preserved.

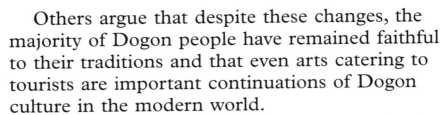

Others argue that despite these changes, the majority of Dogon people have remained faithful to their traditions and that even arts catering to tourists are important continuations of Dogon culture in the modern world.

Many visitors to Dogon country agree that in remote villages, one can still encounter men and women who have the same serenity and peace found in the poses of Dogon art.

It is hoped that such rich and sophisticated traditions as those of the Dogon will continue.▲

Glossary

Amma Dogon god of creation.

anthropocentrism The idea that human beings are the centerpiece of all creation.

Ark of the World In the Dogon creation story, a boat believed to have been sent down from heaven by the creator, Amma, for the creation of the earth.

avatar An incarnation in human form.

benne so (**side speech**) The first of the two intermediate stages in the Dogon order of knowledge.

Big Bang theory The idea that the universe originated billions of years ago as a result of a violent explosion from a point source.

bolo so (**back speech**) The second of the two intermediate stages in the Dogon order of knowledge.

dege Expressive images or sculptures.

dualism The idea that everything in existence comes in pairs or twins that unite opposites.

dynamism The idea that the universe is a system of forces.

egg of the world The oval-shaped mass of matter in which, according to the Dogon creation story, all things in the universe were formed.

fonio A kind of grain.

gin na Big house.

giri so (**front speech**) Elementary knowledge of the world; the first stage in the Dogon order of knowledge.

Hogon semidivine priest-ruler of associated groups of Dogon villages.

Mande An ethnic cluster comprising about 44 separate peoples in West Africa.

microcosmicism The idea that everything in the universe is a miniature of the whole.

Nommo The godly ancestors of human beings; heaven.

nyama Vital force, believed to sustain all life.

ozu tonolu Zigzag line.

Sigui Elaborate ceremony held every sixty years for the renewal of the world.

Sirius A The brightest star in the sky; in Dogon belief, the point at which the universe originated.

Sirius B Smaller but heavier star in orbit around Sirius A.

so dayi **(clear speech)** Advanced knowledge arrived at through progressive initiation and revelation.

Tellem Culture of the medieval inhabitants of Dogon country.

togu na Great shelter.

Toloy culture of the earliest known inhabitants of what is now Dogon country.

yala Images, drawings, or "written signs" in the egg of the world, which defined the identity of things.

For Further Reading

Ezra, Kate. *The Art of the Dogon: Selections from the Lester Wunderman Collection.* New York: The Metropolitan Museum of Art, 1988.

Forde, Daryll, ed. *African Worlds.* Oxford: Oxford University Press, 1954.

Griaule, Marcel. *Conversations with Ogotemmeli: An Introduction to Dogon Religious Ideas.* Introduction by Germaine Dieterlen. London: Oxford University Press for the International African Institute, 1965.

Griaule, Marcel, and Dieterlen, Germaine. *The Pale Fox.* Chino Valley, AZ: Continuum Foundation, 1986.

Imperato, Pascal James. *Historical Dictionary of Mali.* Metuchen, NJ: Scarecrow Press, 1977.

Pern, S. *Masked Dancers of West Africa: The Dogon.* Amsterdam: Time-Life Books, 1982.

Roy, Christopher. *The Dogon of Mali and Upper Volta.* Munich: Fred und Jens Jahn Gallery, 1983.

Index

A

adenine, 30

aduno tal (egg of the world), 25

Amma (Creator), 19, 30, 37, 40

Amma Seru (ancestor), 33, 46

anthropocentrism, 37, 39

Ark of the World, 31

art, 9, 54

astronomy, 50–51

B

benne so (side speech), 36

Big Bang theory, 25, 50

Binu (totemic cult), 41, 43

Binu Sera (ancestor), 33, 46

blacksmith, 15, 31, 55–56

   Master, 33

bolo so (back speech), 36

C

Christianity, 21, 55

chromosome, 25–26, 30

Copernicus, Nicolaus, 51

cytosine, 30

D

dege (wooden status), 9, 37, 40, 41

Dieterlen, Germaine, 28

dualism, 37, 39

dynamism, 37

Dyongu Seru (ancestor), 33, 43, 46

F

farmers, grain, 9

fonio (smallest grain seed), 14, 24

French rule, 21–23

G

Galileo, 50–51

ganna duge (world in harmony), 31

genetic code, 30

ginna (big house), 12

ginna bana (patriarch), 12

giri so (frong speech), 35

grain, spiritual importance of, 13

Griaule, Marcel, 23, 28, 36

guanine, 30

H
Hogon, 14, 48–49
houses, human-shaped, 12
human shape, world created
    in, 26–27

I
iconography, 53
imina (mask cult), 9, 41, 42
    54
Islam, 23, 55

L
leatherworking, 15
Lébé (earth deity cult), 41, 43
Lébé Seru (ancestor), 33, 46

M
Mande, 17, 19, 20, 41
mangu (interdependence), 15
metal casting, 15
microcosmicism, 37, 40

N
Nommo (agents of
    Creation), 16, 30, 33,
    48, 54
nyama, 37, 39, 40, 54

O
Ogotemmeli, 36
origins, 17–20
ozu tonnolo (zigzag line), 39

P
philosophy, 35–40

R
religion, 40–41
renewal, rites of, 41

S
seed of the world, 24–25
Sigui ceremony, 43
so dayi (clear speech), 35,
    36, 37, 53

T
technology, 52–53
Tellem, 19–20
thymine, 30
togu na (meeting place), 12
twinship, 12, 40

V
villages, patrilineal, 10

W
weaving, 19
wood sculpture, 15, 54
world, organization of,
    45–46
worldview, 9, 20–21

Y
yala (code of life), 27–28,
    30, 53

A<small>CKNOWLEDGMENTS</small>

Extensive use has been made in this book of the version of the Dogon creation myth published by Marcel Griaule and Germaine Dieterlen in their contribution "The Dogon" in *African Worlds*, ed. Daryll Forde (1954). For this and for information derived from other works, I am deeply grateful. The sources I consulted must, however, be acquitted of any responsibility for the reinterpretation of Dogon cosmobiological ideas in view of the scientific ideas and "discoveries" of the 20th century. On Dogon arts and architecture, I am especially indebted to the special edition of *African Arts* (1988) devoted to the Dogon.

A<small>BOUT THE</small> A<small>UTHOR</small>

Currently Chair of the Department of Africana Studies at the University of Massachusetts, Boston, Chukwuma Azuonye earned a B.A. summa cum laude in English literature at the University of Nigeria, Nsukka, and a Ph.D. in African literature from the School of Oriental and African Studies, University of London. In 1988-89, he participated in founding the Center for Igbo Studies at the Imo State University, Okigwe, and he held a Fulbright Senior Fellowship in the Department of Folklore and Folklife, University of Pennsylvania (1991-92). His poetry, short stories, and numerous scholarly papers and monographs have been published in journals in Africa, Europe, and the Americas.

E<small>DITOR</small>

Gary Van Wyk, Ph.D.

P<small>HOTO</small> C<small>REDITS:</small> Cover, pp. 11 (bottom left), 22, 29, 44 © Phyllis Galembo; pp. 8, 16, 27, 38 © Eliot Elisofon/Eliot Elisofon Photographic Archives; pp. 11 (top), 14, 32, 34, 49, 56 © Jeffrey Jay Foxx; pp. 11 (bottom right), 13, 20 © Herbet M. Cole; pp. 43, 47, 57 © A. Lorgnier/VISA/ GLMR/Gamma Liaison

D<small>ESIGN:</small> Kim Sonsky